ENJOY!.

Bill

The 24-CARROT MANAGER

The 24-CARROT MANAGER

A remarkable story
of how a leader
can unleash
human potential

ADRIAN GOSTICK
& CHESTER ELTON

WITH A FOREWORD BY
BILL JOHNSON

Gibbs Smith, Publisher

First Canadian English Edition

06 05 04 03   5 4 3 2 1

Text © 2002 by O. C. Tanner Recognition Company

Foreword © 2003 by O. C. Tanner Recognition Company

Published by
Gibbs Smith, Publisher
P.O. Box 667, Layton, Utah 84041

Orders: (1-801) 544-9800
www.gibbs-smith.com

Designed and produced by Gotham Design/NYC
Printed and bound in the U.S.A.

ISBN 1-58685-402-X

"As a harried and results-pressed businessman, work life is all about return on investment (ROI). After sinking my scarce time into a book, I do a rough ROI calculation by asking two questions: "Is this really going to build my business?" and "How rough a slog was the book to get through?" *The 24-Carrot Manager* might be my highest ROI book ever. I think it'll have big impact on my company... and it's a blast of fresh air to read."

Cliff Clive
President, Roche Consumer Health North America

"In *The 24-Carrot Manager*, Gostick and Elton have redrawn the boundaries on how executives should use rewards and recognition to unleash their organization's human potential. This easy-to-read book gives a 360-degree view of all the recognition tools available to us. We have no more excuses for not using them!"

Jean-Luc Butel
President, Independence Technology,
a Johnson & Johnson Company

"What a delight! *The 24-Carrot Manager* is the natural sequel and complement to *Managing with Carrots*. Where *Managing with Carrots* is a 'what to' recognition book, *The 24-Carrot Manager* gives us a comprehensive 'how to' recognize employees—chock full of good-for-everyone carrot recipes."

Debra Sikanas
Baudville, Inc., and President of the National
Association for Employee Recognition

For our
moms and dads,
who were
our first bosses

Joan and Gordon Gostick

Irene and Dalton Elton

CONTENTS

ACKNOWLEDGEMENTS

Special thanks to:

Our colleagues
- Kent Murdock
- David Sturt
- Tim Treu
- Cheryl Kerzner
- Gary Beckstrand and the Entrada Team
- Greg Boswell
- Lori Janes-Young
- Cordell Clinger

Our friends and contributors
- Bill Johnson
- Lauren Orsini
- Christie Giles
- Randall Shirley

Our designer
- Richard Sheinaus/Gotham Design, NYC

Our publishers
- Christopher Robbins
- Madge Baird
- Gibbs and Catherine Smith

The people and companies quoted within.

By Bill Johnson
President and Chief Executive Officer, McDonald's Canada

SOMETIMES I FEEL LIKE the luckiest guy in the world! Not only am I blessed with a wonderful family and friends, but I have also spent my entire professional career working for one of the best companies in the world—McDonald's.

When I was a teenager, I began my first job at McDonald's in London, Ontario. At the time, I wanted to earn some extra spending money and meet new friends. Little did I know that I would be heading down an exciting career path with unimagined possibilities for growth.

Over the past twenty-five years, my McDonald's career has taken me many places and taught me many things, including the value of people to an organization.

At McDonald's, we believe that people are the heart and soul of our business. From the crew who serve our customers every day, to our franchisees whose entrepreneurial spirit and energy brings our brand to life in their communities, to our network of leading

Canadian suppliers—it's the people who make McDonald's special.

McDonald's founder Ray Kroc was an exceptional man who, in many ways, was ahead of his time in terms of his business philosophies. One of Ray's most famous quotes, "None of us is as good as all of us," underscored his belief in a team approach. Ray believed that rewarding your people was one of the most important investments you can make in your business.

Ray cast a strong and compelling shadow that is still felt at McDonald's today. Our strong record of employee retention demonstrates that our employees feel valued and motivated to stay on and grow with us. Approximately 50 percent of our McDonald's restaurant managers started as crew and more than 65 percent of our senior management team began their careers just like I did, serving McDonald's customers at the front counter.

At McDonald's, we reward our people in many ways. We have formal recognition programs at every level of the organization that reward individual results, commitment, new thinking and teamwork, as well as career milestones. However, we believe that "carrots" come in many forms that fall outside these structured programs. We believe that treating employees with respect, communicating openly, celebrating successes and saying 'thanks for a job well done' are the cornerstones of recognition.

Let me give you a quick example. In 1980, I was fortunate to be one of McDonald's Canada's first recipients of the President's Award, given to the top 1 percent of McDonald's employees world-wide. Our then president and McDonald's Canada founder, George Cohon, called me into his office to tell me the great news. I can honestly say that George's words of encouragement and his personal congratulations meant more to me than the award itself!

Today, in my role as Chairman, I take every opportunity to visit restaurants across the country and interact with the men and women who make up our Canadian system. I continue to be inspired by the pride and enthusiasm that exists within our Canadian McFamily. But we must do more. We must put as much effort into celebrating and rewarding our people as we place on other areas of our business. By celebrating employees, we boost their morale and ensure overall satisfaction, which has a direct impact on our customers' experience. Employees are our front line ambassadors—it is their faces and voices that represent McDonald's to our customers. A positive attitude and a friendly smile speak volumes about our company.

In this book, Adrian Gostick and Chester Elton have done an outstanding job at building a case for recognition as a vital part of your business plan. In an easy-to-read and entertaining way, you will find many simple and straightforward tips for using "carrots" to ensure your organization stays healthy!

Reading this book is a great step toward becoming a better manager and helping lead your organization in a new direction. I sincerely wish all of you many rewards—both personal and professional—as you aspire to be a true "24 carrot manager."

Bill Johnson

The 24-CARROT MANAGER

INTRODUCTION

WHEN I (CHESTER) WAS A BOY, we lived in Vancouver, British Columbia. One day I was walking in a downtown park with my father. A homeless woman was pushing a cart toward us, and as she passed she dropped something. My father bent down, picked up the item, handed it to her, and held her by the arm for a moment. Then, in his characteristic way, he said something that made her laugh.

Without a doubt, he made her day. But as we walked away, my eight-year-old sensibilities were horrified. "Dad," I whispered, "You shouldn't talk to those kind of people."

My father smiled and said something I will always remember: "Chester, be kind to everyone—everyone's having a hard day."

What a simple, profound lesson. You never know when your kind word or act will make a difference in someone's life. As managers, we must always assume "everyone's having a hard day." We cannot afford to do any less. In fact, we've got to do a whole lot more ... because we control the office carrot supply.

And carrots can change everything.

Carrots, in our terms, are effective rewards and recognition. Whether you know it or not, it's what your employees are craving. And it's that hunger for recognition that drives them to leave for other jobs—searching for greener pastures where they will feel needed and appreciated. To hold onto them and keep them committed, you've got to create a carrot culture, a work team where people come first and where the good days out-number the bad.

Unfortunately, as managers, carrots rarely cross our minds. We traditionally spend most of our time worrying about our products or our customers or our bosses' whims, and very little time worrying about what's really important: the people who keep our businesses going—our faithful employees.

As one senior leader of a supermarket chain recently told us, "[In our company], we put people in positions of authority who have no right being there. They end up spending most of their time worrying about what headquarters thinks. Not one in ten understands that their most important responsibility is to moti-vate and energize the people who work for them."

The fact is, we've been buying into the traditional corporate management gobbledygook for so long, we've not only forgotten how to give recognition, but *many of us don't even remember what a real carrot looks like.* As a result, we're starting to experience the first signs of recognition deficiency: acceptance of the status quo.

The majority of managers have little hope that anything could coax more ideas, efficiency and productivity out of their staffs. They have given up on trying to help employees gain a better understanding of what is expected of them. Most of us don't believe it's in our power to develop more loyalty and commitment in our truly outstanding people.

Some of us have even progressed to the advanced stages of recognition deficiency. We're the ones who never have been given real carrots ourselves—which often can be traced back to our upbringing or our past workplaces.

I (Chester) was talking with my son in his room recently. As I wished him a good night, I said, "I love you, Carter."

"Yeah," he replied. "I know."

I asked, "Why do you think I love you so much?"

His response was profound: "Because your dad loved you."

In short, if we've received praise and recognition as a kid, or a manager in our past has lavished appreciation and recognition on us, we are more likely to share it with our employees. And when we do recognize our employees, they will take that experience with them for the rest of their working careers.

Those of us who didn't grow up with praise or have never received much praise from a boss have no idea that it's even important to pass recognition on to our employees. And when we don't give carrots, we end up with apathy, low morale and turnover.

CHALLENGE:

Think of the last time you were *publicly* recognized by your direct supervisor. Chances are, it's been too long.

Why Turnover Isn't Healthy

We all lose people. It's a fact of business. Even in the worst economic times, the average employee turnover in North America stands at about 20 percent,[1] and just about every company we talk to says that retention of valuable employees (especially after layoffs) is a "critical" issue for their firm. But research shows that up to three quarters of workers don't feel committed to their organizations and don't plan to stay for more than a couple of years.[2]

Most of us never compute the actual costs of losing our truly talented people—those who add real value. Companies that do the math find the financial loss is staggering.

First, they lose the intellectual capital that walks out the door. Then they pay a recruiter to find a new body. Then they might pay for sign-on bonuses, relocation costs and training—not to mention the fact that the new worker might not be as productive as the replaced employee for a few months (or even years) from their hire date. Now, consider the following intangible cost: When your most valuable people leave, you are losing your shining examples, which inevitably causes the remaining troops to wonder, "What's happening to this place? Why are we losing all the best people?"

Of course, many managers try to sugarcoat the problem by preaching that turnover can be a positive thing. "We'll bring in some new blood and generate new ideas." That theory might hold water if your poor performers were leaving. Unfortunately, it's rarely the simple-minded or constant complainers who jump ship. It's your stars, your innovators, your customer-relations heroes. The people who make magic happen in your department or company. The people with options.

So how do you keep them? We'll give you one guess: Carrots.

Forget about golden handcuffs. Carrots—in the form of rewards and recognition—make it hard for employees to pull up roots and move to another company. Face it, most people can give up a corner office with a window without a lot of heart-burn. They won't bat an eye while swapping one benefit plan for another. They'll even sacrifice a company car or a nice office. But they won't part with appreciation and rewards. Carrots are more addicting than potato chips—and without the added fat.

Says Daniel Horne, chairman of the marketing department at Providence College, "There are some relatively inexpensive things that help create the kind of workplace that people do not want to leave. There are very real and psychic costs associated with leaving a job, and the more social ties that exist, the greater those costs will be." [3]

But very rarely do we find leaders who consider recognition to be an initiative worthy of much thought. The result? Here's what we found in one small natural resources company in the Northwest. A new marketing specialist had come on board a few months earlier and was turning heads with his fresh ideas and enthusiasm. It was obvious this man was a top performer who found ways to add value, so we asked him why he'd left his old post at his former company.

He admitted that the money wasn't that much better at his new company, and he had to move his family more than a thousand miles for the new position. But he felt the opportunities were better there. Over an hour-long discussion, we discovered the core of what he was really feeling. At one point he spoke about his former employer passionately: "We had a backyard conservation project going. It was a big deal to the company, and I was able to get them a spot on Oprah's talk show to promote it. Well, the spot came and went. It went off very well. The program looked very good, which made the bosses look good. But I didn't even get a thank-you. It was as if they were embarrassed to acknowledge my good work."

This outstanding marketing guy had left his company largely because his manager would not tell him he was special. No one had told him they wanted him to stay. No one had recognized his unique and valuable contributions. And so they lost him. Not a big surprise.

Some well-considered carrots could have changed all that.

Unfortunately, it's not an isolated problem. Rick Beal, a senior consultant with Watson Wyatt, says that only 24 percent of managers surveyed in a year 2000 study were strategically using rewards as a means of engaging workers to improve performance or reduce turnover. "Notwithstanding the current slowdown, the tight labor market demands that employers be more aggressive and creative with their rewards programs if they want to win the war for talent," added Beal.[4]

In the war of the workplace, many companies are already in full retreat. That's because, after years of driving their troops forward using fear and intimidation, workers aren't willing to fight the battle anymore.

And it *is* a battle zone out there. With layoffs, downsizings, restructurings, and the resulting human toll, the work world is

Let Them (All) Eat Carrots   Top performers aren't the only ones who care about recognition. Carrots can improve profitability and productivity within your entire work team by leaps and bounds. (Just take a look at what that little orange veggie does for rabbits.)

"Leaders must not only understand the necessity to encourage, inspire and reward that top 20 percent, [they must] be sure that the high-performance 70 percent is always energized to improve and move upward," Jack Welch, formerly of GE, recently told his shareholders.[6]

Deep down, most of us know that employee recognition is important. In fact, about half the managers in one study said that recognizing employee achievement is as effective, and often more so, than the work environment itself, pay, and other employee benefits.[7] And when asked which factor is most important in fostering employee satisfaction, leaders from some of the country's 1,000 largest companies ranked "praise and recognition" at the top.

Remember those old Popeye cartoons? (I'll bet you never dreamed you were getting your first lessons in management over your breakfast cereal.) When Popeye ate his spinach, nothing could stop him. Carrots can have a similarly dramatic impact on employee attitude and performance (minus the bulging forearms). Give employees the recognition they need and then step aside and watch the impossible turn into the probable.

becoming increasingly ugly. According to a recent story in the *New York Times*,[5] nearly a quarter of all American workers have been driven to tears by the stress of work. Nearly half describe

Experts in human motivation have been seeing it for more than fifty years. In fact, in 1949, Lawrence Lindahl asked employees to rank the rewards of their jobs. Then he asked managers to rank what they thought employees wanted.[8]

Managers were convinced that employees would put good wages and job security at the top of the list. They were wrong. Number one on the employees' lists was feeling appreciated. Number two was feeling "in" on things. In fact, when employees felt recognized and involved, they were much less likely to worry about money and job security.

But that was then and this is now. Would you put money on different results if that survey took place in today's workplace? Well, the survey *was* repeated in the 1990s. And the results were exactly the same. It seems some things never change.

In fact, in our current economy, equitable rewards and recognition are the most essential elements of a healthy company, according to the American Psychological Association (*Workforce* magazine, July 2000).

That means it may actually be possible to improve the productivity and morale of the majority of our workforce while retaining our top performers. And there's a bonus: the amount of recognition and validation you offer to your employees may be the one thing in your work life over which you have complete and utter control.

When you think about it, carrots are *the* ultimate power lunch.

their office as a place of verbal abuse and yelling. One-third of us routinely find ourselves too stressed to sleep.

Years ago, workers would set up pickets outside the factory.

But this is a new world. In the words of modern philosopher Homer Simpson, "If you don't like your job, you don't strike. You just go in every day and do it half-assed. It's the American way."

Indeed, our troops either tune out or leave the ranks to join a growing number of recruits at firms that lead with carrots.

Of course, we know you. You're the type of kid who slipped his veggies to the dog under the dinner table. And there was that time you dished them onto your baby sister's plate when your mom wasn't looking. (Ever wonder how that sister made it to the senior ranks of a *Fortune* 500 company? Better eating habits maybe?)

That carrot phobia probably stuck with you into adulthood. Up until now, you may have believed you didn't like carrots. You may have thought recognition took too much time and wasn't worth the effort. Maybe you assumed that it was sissy stuff or that it didn't work.

Well, it's time you learned to like your veggies—or at least your carrots. Because they're good for you ... and your employees ... and your company's bottom line.

Who knows, you might discover you like the taste of success.

The 24-CARROT MANAGER

SPACE *to* GROW

CAPTAIN VEX WASN'T HAVING A GOOD WEEK.

It had started out promising. After twenty years of toil and effort, he'd finally been made a station commander. It should have been the proudest, most triumphant day of his life. But instead of loading his duffle with sunscreen for an exotic alien beach, or carefully folding his dress uniform for high-powered powwows on a distant world, he'd been stuffing his bag with cans and cans of Giant Screaming Roach Repellant. That could mean only one thing: Planet Purgatory.

Oh, that wasn't the planet's real name; but it should have been. Colony Sub 3 was about as close as you could get to "you-know-where" without actually dying.

Vex just didn't get it. After all his outstanding work, they'd sent him to the dustiest, drabbest, most I'd-rather-be-boiled-alive-than-live-there planet in the universe. It was absolutely the last place a new commander wanted to go.

"Vex," his commanding general had said, "we're sending you to Sub 3—to work on the colonization."

Captain Vex had released a long, sad breath as the general rubbed her chin and looked the other way.

"Now, I won't lie to you, man," the general added matter-of-factly. "We've sent commanders there before . . . good men and women. But they've all been about as effective as water wings on a sinking submarine, if you get my drift. So, I'm not expecting a lot. Just give it a try."

Captain Vex had opened his mouth, about to release the flood of questions brewing inside, but before he could speak the general snapped a quick salute and disappeared into her office. Vex watched the door slide shut. He looked at the general's secretary, who smiled sadly at him. Vex had no choice but to turn and walk quietly to the intergalactic shuttle, not exactly sure how he would achieve this goal, not sure why the others had failed, and not sure where to even begin.

There he was, two days later in his new assignment, sitting at a dusty desk and looking out a dusty window at the yellow fields of dusty Sub 3. He took a mental note of things.

First, Sub 3 was dusty. A fine film covered everything and made the whole base look like nothing had changed—or for that matter, even moved—for a hundred years. He rubbed a circle of the window pane clean and watched a transport driving past. Dust swirled behind the wheels and quickly settled in the tracks, covering every trace that the truck had ever been there. "Just like any progress I might make," he said out loud to no one.

Second, there were Giant Screaming Roaches. He'd already seen one that was bigger than a Volkswagen from the olden days. He'd taken to sleeping in the bathtub so they wouldn't crawl over him at night.

But, on the positive side, the pay was fine—comparable to anywhere else. And there were some nice perks: they had the same leave as everyone else; they had an inexpensive cafeteria that served synthetic, albeit rubbery, meals at the push of a button; they even had a Casual Friday policy.

Yet even with the pay and perks, the colony had never taken off. Things had just sort of limped along, despite the best efforts of some "darn fine" previous commanders. Settlers and station officers came, and usually left. Only a handful of families had stuck it out from the beginning. And Captain Vex had been warned that they were "the type that couldn't survive on more competitive planets."

Vex scratched his head and opened the top desk drawer. Inside, he pushed aside a pile of gum wrappers and an empty can of bug repellant. The drawer was otherwise empty. He closed it and slid open the bottom drawer. It also appeared empty. He almost closed it before he noticed, in the back, under a thick layer of gray dust, two small envelopes. He picked one up and blew off what must have been years worth of accumulated dust.

"Hmm—" he mumbled, "seeds."

He blew again, taking off the last of the dust. The small package contained carrot seeds, or at least they appeared to be carrot seeds, if you could trust the small orange carrot on the

envelope cover. He turned the package over in his hands. It had obviously never been opened. But it was no wonder. He looked out the window at the yellow, sad-looking fields of Sub 3. It would be hard to grow carrots in that ground. Chances are, nobody had even tried. And just as likely, nobody on this planet had even tasted real vegetables in years. All the cafeteria served was vitamin- and mineral-enhanced synthetic mush that appeared at the push of a button.

He tossed the seeds into the drawer and left for his first assignment.

But all day long, Vex's mind kept returning to those seeds. Who had put them there? He'd never known anyone who had actually planted a garden, although he'd read about people doing it long ago, decades before planet colonization. There had been times in planet Earth's history when people had actually survived on organic food—and liked it . . . a lot. How long had those seeds sat there collecting dust?

At dinnertime, he ordered synthetic carrots. As he ate, he gnawed on a crazy idea. What if he planted those seeds? He ran a napkin over his spoon, wiping the dust away, and smiled wryly. Less than thirty-six hours here, and he was already losing his mind. It was a wild idea. Still, as he crawled into the bathtub that night and drifted off to sleep, the last thought in his mind was, "What would it hurt to try?"

"My back, that's what hurts," he grumbled late the next morning as he stumbled in from planting the seeds.

Planting was hard work. Plus, he'd been fighting the nagging feeling that he was probably doing it wrong. And even if by some miracle he got the planting right, there was a chance that the old seeds wouldn't amount to anything anyway. "Maybe I'm wasting my time," he wondered out loud. "Why go to all this trouble for nothing?"

He sat down and rubbed his chin. Still, if they did actually grow . . .

He wondered about the taste of real organic food. He smiled wryly and thought:

23

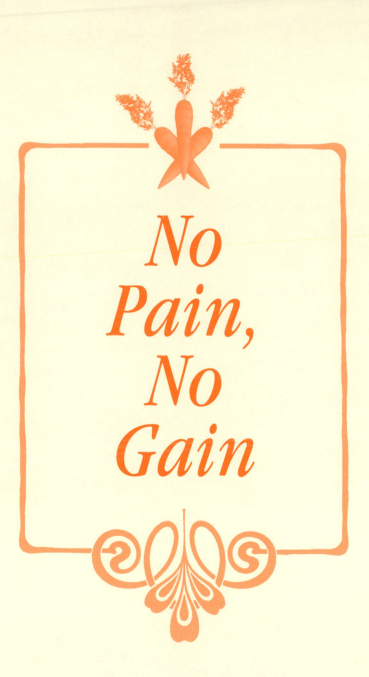

No Pain, No Gain

No Pain, No Gain

Giving your first carrot to an employee might make you feel a bit out of place. And actually, that's good. It means you're gaining ground.

The truth is, most managers are seriously out of practice in presenting employee rewards and recognition. And that's too bad, because managers are the only ones who can.

It's not up to your CEO or corporate culture. Managers are the ones who actually *build* a carrot culture of employee awards and recognition. It's a hard fact of life: To improve their productivity, to enhance their satisfaction, employees need recognition from *you.* Research shows that people accept praise and direction significantly better from their immediate supervisor than from a senior leader who they may see a couple of times a month.

With so much resting squarely on your shoulders, you're bound to feel a little pain. But hang in there, you'll be amazed at what there is to gain. Carrots really are the key to success. Not just in a perfect world. Not in a made-up world. In the real world. In *your* world.

Vegephobia *(The Fear of Carrots)*

Even if you've landed in a hard, unyielding corporate environment. Even if every other manager before you has failed miserably. Even if your employees are so resistant to change, they're gathering dust. Even if your senior leaders believe that recognition comes in the form of a paycheck every two weeks. Even if you've just come through a miserable downsizing. Even if ... (anything else you can think of) ... carrots are the most effective way to make your team better.

Unfortunately, few managers clear time on their plate for recognition.

When we consult with an organization, we typically ask: "What percent of your managers would you say effectively recognize and reward their people?" No matter the industry, just about every client answers: "Probably between 10 and 20 percent."

To effectively manage people, you must give a piece of yourself. You must truly listen, encourage, and be an important part of your employee's work experience.

Why don't more managers recognize their people? We hear a lot of reasons. Here are the most common:

- *I don't want to get too familiar with my employees.*
  Some managers worry that if they are too supportive, too warm and fuzzy, it'll be hard to dispense discipline when needed, or employees will lose respect for them. Our typical response is: "Are you kidding? Do you think your people will

really work harder for someone who is distant and aloof?" Research shows that people work best for managers who seem to care about them and are attentive to their needs. Our question: Why was that research even necessary?

- ***What's in it for me?*** Some managers still wonder about the payoffs of rewards and recognition. According to the largest study ever conducted on workplace satisfaction, recognition and rewards are core essentials of work teams that have high employee productivity, great customer satisfaction and low turnover.[9] In other words, recognition and rewards are not just corporate niceties. It's just about impossible to get great results without consistent, meaningful recognition.

- ***I don't have time.*** We don't doubt that managers are busy. With increased workloads and the decline in support staffs, it seems that today we all have three or four jobs (for which we receive just one paycheck). But recognition should not take an inordinate amount of your time. The authors of this book each manage teams of six or more people; but we take time out to recognize employees because it leads to higher produc-tivity, better workplaces, and, as corny as it sounds, it really *is* the right thing to do.

- ***I don't want to play favorites.*** Some managers are worried about creating "fair-haired boys" on their teams or leaving someone out. Some managers decide instead to "recognize everyone" as a group. This is misguided leadership. These managers not only end up alienating the stars who make a difference, but *reinforcing* the behavior of their average and poor performers. Instead of serving up mass-produced, generic-label carrots to your work group, try this: Put together a chart of all your people and recognize one person in each weekly staff meeting until you have publicly recognized them all. Don't just recognize for "overall greatness" (we'll talk more about this later) but for specific behaviors that are important to your organization. When you start recognizing, you'll be amazed at how easy it is and how nobody feels left out. You'll also find yourself recognizing faster—on the spot—for the "right" behaviors. In most cases, you'll also notice your employees recognizing each other and vying for more of your recognition.

- *They'll be suspicious of my motives.* Some leaders who have tried recognition complain that one or two of their people think they are insincere when they offer praise or rewards. Often we find that the way recognition is handled is a large part of the problem. In one case, we heard about an "ungrateful" employee publicly praising herself before the bosses could and then being suspicious of her manager's later praise. We taught the managers to make recognition events more timely, and to add specific praise with stories, and remarkably the problem evaporated. In fact, there are ways to correct most recognition difficulties with the general ideas we give in this book. Still, we admit that there is a small percentage of the human race who refuse to be satisfied, no matter how sunny their boss may be treating them. As harsh as it sounds, at some point you must determine if these people are harming your efforts as a manager and if they really fit in with your team's culture.

- *The activity will lose meaning.* We often ask managers this question: "Do you tell your wife you love her (your husband you love him)?" They usually answer in the positive. We then say, "And you probably say it just about every day." They nod again. We then ask, "Why?" The managers typically say: "Because she (he) wants to hear it." And before the words are out of the managers' mouths, the light goes on. As employees, most of us can never receive enough *sincere* recognition. It never seems to lose meaning. Just like we need to eat every day, we need to feel the appreciation of others on a regular basis.

- *They'll take advantage of me.* Oh, brother. Next objection.

- *Other managers aren't doing it.* Exactly our point. And just look where it gets them. Of course, we understand that it's uncomfortable to be the first. Some leaders don't want to be early adopters. Others say they'll only get on board if it

comes from the top down in the form of a corporate program. But real leaders do just what that title implies: they lead.
Sure, in a perfect world, the corporate head office would ship
you a crate of fresh-from-the-farm carrots once a week with all
the tools necessary to do recognition right, and every manager would buy in. And, of course, some great companies do just
that. They provide symbolic informal and formal tools and
hold managers accountable for using those resources (we'll
give a few examples later). But successful companies like
those are rare, and you are probably on your own. Yes, that
will set you up for some comparisons, i.e., "Shirley over in
accounting did the same thing I did and she got a much
better reward." But frankly, most people will appreciate the
carrots they are given. And they'll respect a leader who has
the courage to be outstanding in her field.

- ***They'll ask for more money.*** Actually, just the opposite.
  According to workplace studies, employees who are satisfied
  and appreciated are less likely to keep asking for more money.

- ***They'll expect more recognition.*** Yes, they will. Employees
  eat up carrots. When recognition is provided regularly, people
  will stick around a company for seconds—and thirds—all the
  while turning out increasingly better results. And this is a
  problem?

The old saying "You reap what you sow" is truer today than ever before. Give employees the recognition they want—and they'll produce the results you *need*.

CHALLENGE:

Spend a few minutes thinking about your team.
Are there members you never publicly recognize?
Why not?

Space to Grow

THE NEXT DAY, just as the sun rose above the horizon, Captain Vex watered the garden and the newly planted seeds. He thought about the day when he would be able to harvest the carrots, when he could pull those wonderful orange vegetables out of the ground. Vex had never tasted a real carrot—just the synthesized carrot mush the machine in the cafeteria made. His mouth watered as he thought about eating real, organic food.

As he watered his garden, he glanced around. From the hill, he could see the workplaces of his employees. Lt. Constance Atwork was already up, at the crack of dawn, checking her weather research equipment, analyzing atmospheric conditions. Lt. Atwork was a quiet woman, so he really hadn't learned much about her duties. But as he watched her, he could see that she practiced the precision necessary to be a successful weather researcher—checking and rechecking every piece of equipment several times.

"Very good," said Vex to himself.

The captain looked over at the equipment hut. Lt. Malcolm Tent was just beginning his maintenance work for the day. Lt. Tent was a gruff, seemingly angry man. Frankly, Vex was a little intimidated by him.

Vex watched as Lt. Tent gathered his tools and brushes and loaded them into his vehicle. Tent then drove to Vex's home and stopped.

"That's interesting," Vex muttered.

Lt. Tent looked around at the deserted settlement and then began to brush the atmospheric dust from Captain Vex's vehicle.

"Hmm," said Vex. "I'd wondered why my vehicle didn't gather dust." Tent finished his work and then moved on to Lt. Atwork's vehicle.

Vex didn't remember reading anything about brushing vehicles in Lt. Tent's job description. And he had to admit that it bothered him a little. Not that Lt. Tent was cleaning the vehicle; it bothered him that he'd missed it. He had climbed into his truck every morning on the dustiest planet in the universe and taken it for granted that he could see out his windshield. It had been right in front of his nose . . . and he hadn't seen it. He sighed. Maybe it was true what his grandmother had always said:

Carrots
Improve
Your
Eyesight

Carrots Improve Your Eyesight

A publisher of business magazines recently talked to us about a special employee. This young man had developed a new business channel that brought more than a million dollars in new wealth into his company during a time when some magazines were going under due to slowing ad sales. The publisher was obviously thrilled and called a meeting of his entire team to honor this entrepreneur within his ranks.

"Folks, thanks for taking a couple of minutes out of your busy schedules," said the publisher. "Roger has done some remarkable things lately that have made this company vastly more successful."

The publisher looked around and beamed. "I know many of you have helped on this project. I appreciate your help more than you know. We'll have a celebration for the team next week. But today I want to honor the guy who thought all this up. Come on up, Rog."

The team applauded wildly as Roger stood up and walked to the front of the conference room. The publisher warmly shook Roger's hand and then continued his story.

"I was talking with Roger one day in his work area and I asked what he was working on—first mistake."

Everyone laughed.

"He said he was brainstorming an idea—an idea for our own line of management-development seminars. Well, I thought, 'Great idea, Roger; but it's been done before.'

"But, Roger had a different spin on a time-tested idea. And he kept at me until I understood his vision. As you all know, innovation is one of our values around here—it just might be the most important one. I guess that's why I kept listening ... and listening as Roger kept pitching. And finally Roger began to make sense."

The publisher continued for a couple more minutes. He talked about Roger's leadership in bringing a team together to work on the seminars, about the early risks and obstacles, but mostly about the eventual success of the project.

In short, the publisher told his team a powerful story that related an individual accomplishment to the goals and vision of the company. Our publisher friend was successful because carrots had made his eyesight excellent. He was able to use information he'd gleaned about the employee's accomplishments to weave a wonderful story for coworkers—where he could gain the most impact. (And we'll tell you later how he asked the right questions to find the perfect award.)

Creating this kind of impact is possible. *The key is getting out of your office on a regular basis.*

It's not that hard. Just make sure you spend a small part of every day walking (or driving, if necessary) through your work location, talking to your people. Ask them what they are working on. Ask them what rewards they value.

Some managers make notes for potential recognition stories while they are walking around. Others come back to their offices and enter their thoughts in the computer or a notebook. You might think you'll remember all these details, but you probably won't. And these day-to-day stories are the kind that will add spice to your award and recognition presentations.

And while you are walking around, if you notice something great, say so immediately to the employee. Carrots don't keep well. You'll find employees respond to specific praise given while it's fresh on your mind much better than they do to indifference.

As you walk, notice, too, what people have in their offices, cubicles, trucks or other workspaces. Chances are, the items people display in their personal spaces will give you ideas for personalized recognition awards.

By walking around and recognizing your employees for doing the right things, you help them identify which behaviors should be cultivated and which should be weeded out. Sometimes, the right direction is the only thing employees need to really blossom in their jobs.

Here's a simple example of paying attention. Garrett Boone, CEO of The Container Store, watches weekend store receipts come in on Monday morning and then personally sends handwritten notes of praise to the best-performing managers and staffs. And, if an individual does something remarkable that helps meet the corporate goals, he'll send a companywide voice or email recognizing that person.[10]

Boone says the results of creating this kind of culture speak for themselves. The Container Store's turnover rate is about one quarter of the industry average, sales have typically increased by 20 to 25 percent per year, and in 2001 the company was chosen by *Fortune* as the "Best Company to Work For in America," an honor rarely bestowed on a retail company.

Here's another example from a leader with whom we've done quite a bit of work. He called us in after reaching an epiphany of sorts on how recognition should be strategic.

"It was time for cash bonuses," he told us. "And I sat down with my new account supervisor. He had a list of his people and had ranked them from one to six."

But instead of just signing off on the cash recognition, the leader asked, "So, what's involved in the ranking?"

The supervisor said, "Well, Susan's number one. She gets the new business packets out in the fastest time, and they are always very neat." The leader thought for a moment. "But who gets their packages out in the most creative manner? Who helps us win the most accounts?" he asked.

The supervisor mumbled, "Well, that would be Chris."

Guess where Chris was on the ranking. Near the bottom.

Said the leader to us, "If I had approved the bonuses as is, would we have rewarded the right thing? Of course not. The message we would have sent to Chris would have been work faster, work neater. Follow our procedures. We don't reward creativity. We don't reward new-account people who actually win new accounts."

A carrot culture without defined goals—or worse yet, with *mis*defined goals—will never succeed at juicing the best efforts from employees.

As this leader learned, we cannot afford to confuse activity with achievement. When recognized for the right things—for behaviors that are important to your organization—the people being recognized and their coworkers work smarter. How successful your strategy is depends on how well it is implemented. And that depends on how well your people are treated. The better they are treated, the better they will treat your customers. It's that simple.

CHALLENGE:

Carefully think about what you will recognize in your team.
At your next staff meeting, recognize one person
for living one of these behaviors.
Keep this tradition going by recognizing one person
in every meeting. Encourage your workers to do the same.
Make sure to tie recognition to your company's
goals and values.

SPACE to GROW

A FABLE · Part III

As Vex Walked Back Down to His Office, he began to wonder how he could recognize and thank Atwork and Tent for their efforts. He was allowed to give pay raises and spot cash bonuses. But they just showed up impersonally in their transmissions. He might be able to give an extra day of furlough. But that involved red tape and, anyway, it really wouldn't be that personal. He could wait for their annual review, but that might be months away.

No, he needed something that would be immediate and meaningful to each of them.

He realized the answer wouldn't be easy. He was running from dawn till dusk with all the station responsibilities. But even though it would be hard, he'd have to find the time to talk more with his lieutenants. He would have to get to know them, learn what they valued.

The next day, as Vex was getting his lunch in the cafeteria, he spotted Lt. Atwork and sat down beside her.

"Nice day," said Vex.

"Yes," said Lt. Atwork, barely loud enough for the captain to hear.

"Do you think we'll have more wind today?" Vex asked.

"I shouldn't think so," said the lieutenant. "The low pressure has shifted to the south."

"Well, you would know," said Vex. "You're the expert."

Lt. Atwork smiled back shyly.

They talked for half an hour, and Vex learned that his lieutenant had grown up on a farm in a distant quadrant.

The next day, Captain Vex visited Lt. Tent in his maintenance hut.

"Hello," said Vex as he cautiously entered the hut. "Do you mind if I come in? Won't take long."

Malcolm Tent grunted. He was sprawled under a vehicle that was up on blocks.

"Um . . . well, I just wanted to see if you needed anything," added the captain, a bit awkwardly.

The lieutenant slid out from under the vehicle and stared suspiciously at Vex.

"Anything?" Tent asked.

"Sure."

"Well, as long as you're sending out for supplies, we need some new grub in the mess hall," said Tent. "I'm sick of the same old synthetic stuff."

"Okay. Is that all?"

"Yep." With that, Tent slid back under the vehicle.

The next morning, Captain Vex began pulling the first weeds from among the green carrot shoots now pushing through the ground. He still hadn't thought of a perfect way to recognize the shy Lt. Atwork or the gruff Lt. Tent.

But then, as he stood to look over his new field, the answer suddenly became clear. In fact, the answer was right under his feet.

The perfect way to recognize his people was with carrots—real, fresh vegetables! It was like a voice in his head said:

Pick Your Carrots Wisely

Pick Your Carrots Wisely

When she was first out of college, recognition consultant Kathe Farris began working for a bank. She started near the bottom of the corporate ladder, answering phones. During a promotion to cross-sell mutual funds, she was able to bring a whopping $1.2 million into the bank.

"So what did they give me?" asks Kathe. She scoffs and answers her own question: "A mug."

Kathe shakes her head incredulously: "A mug," she repeats. "Do you think I—or anyone who worked around me—ever sold mutual funds again? Of course not."

Obviously, all carrots are not created equal.

In some cases, a mug would be a fine reward for a simple job well done. It is certainly possible to take an object of little value and make it more valuable. Remember how badly you coveted that gold star in grade school? The star had no value apart from what you and your fellow students gave it. By the same token, wouldn't you prize a handwritten note of appreciation from your boss? We've seen handwritten notes and cards from supervisors posted on hundreds of cubicles and office walls throughout North America. Why? Because the recognition is rare and valuable.

But for Kathe, who had obviously gone above and beyond

what was expected in her position, a mug was a very poor reward. She wanted something lasting to remind her of that remarkable achievement.

We've heard the mug tale more than once. In fact, a very good *Fortune* 100 company called us in after a hideous "mug" fiasco. They wanted to make sure they never repeated the mistake.

This pharmaceutical giant had just won a very rigorous man-ufacturing "quality" award. Hundreds of people had put in over-time, disrupted their personal lives and made numerous sacri-fices over a six-month period to win the award. When the award recipients were announced and the company's name was read, the employees were thrilled.

Company management quickly called the employees to-gether for a celebration. They held the meeting after work, and they kept the reward a mystery. Two shifts gathered in the cafe-teria and the president gave a speech about what a great effort everyone had made and what this award meant to the company, how it tied in so well with their overall drive for quality.

He then concluded with, "To celebrate this great victory, all of you will receive a commemorative gift."

"It's about time," said someone in the back. Everyone laughed. The mood was festive.

Then the CEO nodded and the director of corporate communication pulled a string and unveiled a giant pyramid made out of plastic mugs. The silence that followed was deafening. People were absolutely stunned. It was as if they had unveiled a stack of moldy Christmas fruitcakes.

Finally, a man walked up and took his mug. The CEO was just about to breathe a sigh of relief when the employee shook his head and began to guffaw. Others followed suit. And over the next few weeks, the mug became the new (facetious) symbol of quality in the company.

When the company executives recounted this tale, we had to admit the idea of a timely public celebration was good. The idea of a speech recognizing the accomplishment was wonderful. A commemorative gift could have been a perfect touch. But after months of sweat, effort and sacrifice, the execution was certainly lacking.

The moral of this story is: *To have the intended effect, a reward's value should be an appropriate symbol of the employee's effort and its outcome.* Remember, value isn't the only qualification for an effective award. Just as importantly, the reward should be tangible and memorable. And carrots have to be appropriate for the individual. There are a lot of onions out there masquerading as carrots. And a thoughtless award can leave a bad taste in an employee's mouth.

Here's just such a story of a high-ticket award that just didn't fly.

We once were asked in to a company that was considering taking companywide a seemingly successful sales-performance program they had launched in one division. The winner of the sales contest was presented with a wonderful trip to an exotic locale. In the course of our work, we found that the man had not taken the trip. We asked him why he had not used the seemingly wonderful reward.

"I'm terrified of flying," he replied.

A lot of the time, you can avoid problems like this through frequent department walk-throughs and careful observation and listening. But when in doubt about the appropriateness of an award, ask. Ask the employee's spouse. Ask his coworkers. Ask the employee.

It's easier than you think. Look around your office. Chances are, you've collected things that remind you of what you have accomplished, the people you love, the places you've been. At work, we collect things. We even treasure these things. And we want people to ask about our things. So, go ahead and ask. The time you spend will be worth its weight in employee loyalty, because time and time again, employees attach more value to a reward they find personally meaningful than to a generic gift.

In fact, in a year 2000 survey, 63 percent of North American employees said their loyalty would increase if the employer offered an ongoing incentive program that *allowed employees to choose rewards* that were personally relevant.[11]

Here's a great example. At Long John Silver's restaurant chain, leaders were losing employees at an alarming rate. Turnover in food service is typically 200 percent or higher a year. And, frankly, company leaders were having a tough time getting their frontline workers—typically sixteen- to twenty-one-year-olds—motivated and excited about the company's goals. The carrot they picked was relatively simple. When employees were caught doing something right, they were handed a gold coin. Actually, it was a yellow plastic coin, but they got the idea. When employees collected enough of these golden treasures, they turned them in for hip merchandise.

The result? Restaurants had to re-lacquer the floors because their workers were cleaning them so often, says Linda Nestor, director of compensation of parent company Yorkshire Global Restaurants. As Linda toured the restaurants for feedback, many of these young workers admitted, "Sure, I could get twenty-five cents more an hour over at McDonalds, but I want to get that necklace."

Adds Linda, "One young man I will never forget as long as I live. He was mopping the floor. He told me he was hoping to save up enough coins to get his two-year-old son a basketball goal and ball."

And another plus: Workers were starting to understand what was important to the company—cleanliness, hospitality, accuracy, etc.

Here's yet another great example, albeit at a much grander scale. Remember the publisher whose outstanding employee brought more than a million dollars into the company? Says the publisher, "I called Roger's wife and found out he had always wanted a Breitling watch."

"So you gave him a Breitling?" we asked incredulously.

"No. I *presented* him with a Breitling. It was engraved with a special message, and he cried like a baby."

The publisher smiled to himself and then added, "I could have given him a $3,500 bonus, but do you think he would have wept? Do you think it would have had that kind of impact?"

Next month, when the publisher asks Roger to tackle an impossible project, what response do you think he'll get? That's easy: Roger will walk through fire for his boss. When Roger looks at this watch (which most people do about forty times a day), who do you think will come to his mind?

There's no doubt that finding the right award and planning

an effective recognition presentation takes time. And time is money. But as these and other outstanding managers have found, any moments spent on recognition are well spent.

Carrots consistently yield more than their money's worth in employee retention, dedication, motivation and morale.

One a Week

Five a day. That's how many fruits and vegetables your body needs to keep in top condition. Recognition is much easier. To keep employee morale and motivation going strong, serve up one thoughtful reward (or verbal praise) a week. It'll keep your workforce in peak condition.

Sure, that may seem like a lot of recognition. But it's not as difficult as it might appear at first glance. And we can help. During our work with hundreds of North American companies, we've dug up a list of innovative carrots. When properly aligned with your company vision and goals—and selected for the right employee—these awards and recognition methods can be particularly effective.

Some of these rewards are simple, some rather complex. One question we are often asked is "What performance is worth a big reward versus something simple, like a movie ticket?" The answer is: It depends. It depends on your department and company goals. It depends on the overall contribution of the people you are recognizing. Perhaps they're not all superheroes, but many are vital core performers who come in every day, keep their heads down, and get work done consistently and accurately. Your company needs both types of employees, but their rewards may vary.

Frankly, in the end, the determination of what type of reward is appropriate depends on *you*.

You will have to determine what type of carrot will flourish in your corporate climate. *You* will have to develop your own criteria for tying the size of reward to the actions and value of the individual.

At first, it may not be easy. (That's why so few managers do it.) But the results that grow out of effective recognition can't be reproduced any other way.

Here are some ideas to get your creative thinking started. Remember, not every award will work for every employee or every work culture. Do your homework first.

- Say, "Thank you."
- Send a letter of praise to her spouse/family (this is probably the most powerful, untapped recognition we've seen).
- Volunteer to do his least favorite task.
- Remember their special days (birthdays, anniversaries, etc.) and write a message in a card.

- Gather coworkers to sing a lighthearted rendition of a song such as, "You Light Up My Life," "We Are the Champions," etc.

- Have a department break in honor of her.

- Give him a standing ovation from the entire team.

- Wash her car.

- Give him tickets to the symphony or opera.

- Give her tickets to a ball game.

- Give him a book from his favorite author.

- Let her park in your parking space for a week.

- Give out traveling awards like a rubber chicken or other fun item.

- Organize a department-wide water-gun fight in the parking lot in her honor (on a casual day).

- Give her a gift certificate to a home-improvement store (great for employees who have just moved or recently built a home).

- Bring him a cup of coffee or favorite morning beverage.

- Buy lunch for her and three or four coworkers of her choice.

- Give him a pass for a couple of hours off to attend a child's school activity.

- Give a great new employee a shopping spree to a local store to personalize her office space.

- Give him golf lessons.

- Give her a three-hour maid service.

- Give him movie tickets.

- Give her the latest book that relates to her career.

- Pay for a fitness fanatic's gym membership.

- Give him a box of his favorite chocolate bars or other candy.

- Give her a trip to a day spa.

- Send a handwritten note of praise (not a "thanks for all you do" letter, but a note with specific praise).

- Give him a subscription to his favorite magazine (not just business-related).

- Give her a gift certificate for dinner with her spouse.

- Give him a paid sabbatical to do something in the community, learn a new skill or volunteer with a nonprofit organization.

- Have a recognition box in your office. When someone does something outstanding, let him choose a reward out of the box—everything from a free lunch to an oil change.

- Create a yearbook for your team with pictures and stories of accomplishments during the year.

- Put together a scrapbook of memories for an employee who is celebrating a milestone anniversary. Give each person on the team a blank page to fill out with stories or pictures of their experiences with that employee. Then, after the public recognition moment, the individual has not only a treasured award from the company but something from her coworkers that captures *their* feelings.

- Ask her to be a mentor to a new hire.

- Have a monthly breakfast meeting in an outside location. Invite your team, share ideas and recognize at least one person.

- Bring in a massage therapist with a chair to reward your team.

- Develop a year-end award for those in your department who have gone above and beyond on a consistent basis. In a formal setting, present them with tangible awards that they will value, and offer specific praise.

- Take everyone to an inspirational movie on a Friday afternoon and then send them home early.

- Put up a bulletin board in your department and post letters of thanks from customers (internal and external).

- Deliver candy or other snacks to your troops on a certain day every week. Take the opportunity to learn what your people are working on and recognize their good behavior.

- Interview your people and capture their wisdom. Compile the quotes and stories in a booklet and hand it out to new hires.

- Set department goals for standards, attendance, etc., and present appropriate items with your company logo when employees reach the milestone. For example, a manager at an oil and gas company may present a company jacket when an employee reaches a certain level of expertise. A manager in an insurance business may present a clock with a company emblem to employees who reach a comparable skill level.

- Make your formal anniversary, performance, sales and safety awards as meaningful as possible. Award presentations should be some of the most memorable experiences in your employees' work lives. Done right, they will bond employees to your organization.

Greg Boswell, executive vice president of the National Association for Employee Recognition, is a wonderful practitioner of this type of personalized informal recognition. Greg once managed a staff of six. He now manages one person, and the two of them do the same workload as the much larger department used to do.

"With a declining economy and shrinking staffs, it's more important than ever to recognize those employees who are left," he says. "With my employee, I understand her as an individual and what makes her unique. For example, she loves chocolate chip cookies."

So, when Greg recently went on a week-long business trip and his employee had to pick up the slack, he left her enough money to buy a daily fresh-baked cookie from a nearby vendor.

"She's stuck in the office while I'm traveling, so I want to make sure that every day some recognition is happening and she knows that I appreciate her."

When it was review time, Greg also invited his boss to the meeting so that this senior leader could hear all the good things his employee was doing. And the leader talked to the employee about where the company was going, which, according to Greg, made the employee even more motivated to be a part of that future.

Says Greg, "It does work. The hardest part is actually doing it, saying something, giving something. Just try it once and you'll do it more."

Keep it up, and soon, picking the right carrots will become a piece of cake.

Corporate Carrots

Some managers aren't left alone when it comes to offering rewards and recognition. There are many great companies that have organized informal and formal recognition to great effect. Here are just a few examples of great corporate carrots:

Hoyman, Dobson & Co., a CPA firm in Melbourne, Florida, believes employee rewards can keep employees satisfied and committed, even when they are working hard. That's why the fifty-person firm adopted stress relievers ranging from in-office back massages to giving employees every other Friday off in the summer. Not only that, but employees who go above and beyond and work on Saturdays are supplied with catered full-course luncheons. And lunch is not restricted to the employees; spouses or children sometimes join them. Margaret Jenkins, human resources coordinator for the firm, says whenever she senses a stressful situation in the office, she goes to a nearby Dairy Queen, gets Dilly Bars, and then walks around to everyone's desk, offering a choice of flavors.[12]

Federal Express Corporation (FedEx) offers a Safe Driving Award Program. Drivers who remain free of accidents for at least a year receive awards—from watches to luggage to jewelry—and a 10-karat-gold FedEx emblem. FedEx believes safety is the company's number one priority, and with this powerful recognition program they are directing their people to live this important corporate goal. The result? Since the introduction of the program, company officials say driver safety has increased significantly.

Do something right at the Global Services division of EMC and you'll likely wear the company's appreciation. At this information-storage company headquartered in Massachusetts, employees who go above and beyond in helping the company exceed its goals and sustain a supportive work environment receive a cash bonus and an embroidered apparel item, ranging from a golf shirt to a windbreaker. An online nomination wizard helps nominating employees and managers determine the level of award.

Toronto-based Fairmont Hotels offers its employees a service-award program with heirloom awards and a symbolic gold-and-diamond company emblem. Named recently as one of the best companies to work for in Canada, Fairmont also offers a strategic performance-award system closely tied to the company's mission. The performance system is run not by senior leaders but by committees comprised of 70 percent employees and 30 percent frontline managers from each property. Employees are nominated by fellow employees and guests for a BravoGram, a card of thanks that is then submitted as a nomination for Star of the Month. One or two monthly Stars in each hotel receive a plaque and select a merchandise award. A Star of the Year receives an all-expenses-paid vacation for two to any Fairmont property.[13]

Cash vs. Carrots   After the release of our first book, *Managing with Carrots*, we were fortunate enough to be asked to appear on several national television and radio programs, including a few interviews on Public Radio International's *Marketplace*. My (Adrian's) first interview on *Marketplace* started out quite interestingly.

The reporter, Cash Peters, had enjoyed the book but was troubled by the premise of recognition over cash. His first question hit me right between the eyes: "Are you really saying that someone would turn down a $300,000-a-year job if you gave him a plaque?"

I explained that, of course, we weren't making that claim. A company must pay fair wages. Our book wasn't called *Managing By Carrots Alone.* But we were saying that cash has not been proven to be a consistent motivator. While most companies throw more money at their best people to keep them and keep them committed, research shows that recognition and involvement are the keys to employee satisfaction.

By the end of the interview with Cash, we had reached a mutual understanding. But still he was not completely sold—until his experiment. He tried a few of the ideas in the book on his office staff, and then he asked several people in his office (a very scientific survey) if they would want a job that paid loads and loads of money, or one

Net2000 Communications, a Herndon, Virginia–based provider of broadband telecommunications services, rewards its best employees for their outstanding performance and dedication to success by offering them cars. Through the "Car in Every where they felt appreciated and rewarded.

To Cash's utter dismay, every single person in his office chose the carrot over the cash.

Cash Peters had to admit on air, "Managing with carrots. It works!"

While managers must pay market rates to keep the best people, "American business is fast discovering that monetary rewards are not only very costly, they are extremely limited in their ability to motivate employees," says Wayne Slough of the Center for Organizational Effectiveness at J. Sergeant Reynolds Community College in Richmond, Virginia. "No matter how much money a company might give, employees will soon become 'habituated' to it, and a phenomenon that researchers have termed 'reward inflation' occurs. . . . Failing to meet employee expectations could get an employer eaten alive."[15]

There are other problems with cash. When people are striving for money, they will often take shortcuts to maximize their financial gain, even if it means sacrificing quality.

Wouldn't it be easier to just let them eat carrots? Strange but true: spreading a little of the orange stuff around will give you results that turn other managers green with envy.

Garage" program, the honored employees are permitted to choose either a BMW Z3, BMW 325, Audi TT or Dodge Durango. The first cars were awarded in January 1999 to employees who, according to the company, went the distance and then some. "In the competitive market we are currently facing, this program helps Net2000 continue to recruit and keep top talent," a company official says. Employees are eligible to participate in the program after two years with Net2000. Cars are leased and paid for by the company and given to the employee for a period of three years, with an option to buy at the end of the contract.[14]

CHALLENGE:

When you hire your next employee, say:
"I know you are going to do great things, and I want
to know how to reward you."
Then spend ten minutes learning about his or her interests.
Maybe he likes fishing (half a day off might be a great reward),
the arts (tickets to the symphony), or reading (a book).
Make a note of these interests and then use those interests
to determine what day-to-day rewards you can offer.
Not only will this give you
great ideas for recognition, it will show that you
have interest in them as a person.

SPACE to GROW

A FABLE · Part IV

In a split second, Vex's carrots had transformed from a crazy experiment to something more. Because he had put time, effort and care into growing them, and because fresh food was so rare on this remote world, his carrots would be more valuable to his employees than a standard-issue letter of commendation or another title.

To his knowledge, nothing—let alone carrots—had ever been grown on Sub 3. Because the carrots had become valuable, Vex wanted the moment he presented them to be special. He wanted them to know he had thought of them personally. He wanted them to know that he cared. He began to plan how he'd surprise Tent and Atwork.

It was obvious that Lt. Tent had a passion for food. He'd asked for new synthesized selections when Vex sent for supplies. Vex decided he'd publicly present Lt. Tent with a plate of fresh carrots—covered in butter. Then he'd thank him for his attention to detail—detail that made Sub 3 a good place to live and work.

As for Lt. Atwork, she was a little shy and might not appreciate a public gathering. As for the award: she had grown up on a farm. Perhaps she might not mind joining him in the garden for a few minutes, helping him pull the first few carrots out of the ground. Then, for the real reward, he could present her with a bundle of the valuable carrots and mention that her efforts beyond the call of duty had not gone unnoticed.

....

Within a few weeks, the carrots were ready.

He knocked on Lt. Atwork's door.

"I was hoping you could join me this afternoon," he said. She nodded, expecting they would be conducting weather experiments. "Um . . . I was hoping you would help me harvest the carrots."

The lieutenant was a little surprised by the invitation. And when they began working, their conversation was a little awkward at first.

"I certainly have appreciated your dedication to our weather research," said Vex. "I know you put in long hours with your instrumentation and analysis, and it is a big help to our work here. My reports to headquarters are much more detailed because of your contributions. I was hoping you'd accept some of the carrots as a reward for your wonderful efforts."

Lt. Atwork left with a big bundle of carrots, and a bigger smile. She seemed genuinely pleased with the fresh carrots and the compliments. Next time he might be able to try complimenting her in public.

Lt. Malcolm Tent would be a little harder, thought the captain. But Tent accepted the invitation to a recognition event and just as eagerly accepted his praise and carrots. In front of a group of his peers, Lt. Tent took the plate of carrots and lifted one of the orange vegetables to his lips. He took a tentative bite and his eyes lit up. "I haven't had grub like this in years," he said.

"Well, I'm glad I could make it for you," said the captain. "I wanted to reward you and let you know that

CARROTS

I notice your attention to detail." Vex turned to the group. "We all know about the dust around here. Well, a couple of weeks ago, early one morning, I noticed Lt. Tent cleaning the dust off my vehicle. Apparently he does it for all of us before we wake up, making our work lives a little bit better and our station a little bit more presentable. Since then, I've seen that Lt. Tent approaches all of his work with that level of dedication. Frankly, most of the things he does, no one ever thanks him for. But today, we thank you."

They shook hands warmly and the group applauded. Lt. Tent blushed and ate a few more carrots.

With each recognition presentation, Captain Vex felt more at home giving carrots. In fact, he was a little sad when he pulled the last plant from the ground. He hadn't realized how much he enjoyed giving those carrots away, looking for the right person, the right time, the perfect words.

Just then, Vex remembered a remote conference he had once attended. He had been part of a delegation that had traveled to form a treaty with the hostile Tweebs. At that time, the general had worried over every detail. The general had prepared his words carefully before they landed, and when the delegation did step off the shuttle, the general had presented the Tweeb leader with a beautiful memento of the occasion.

Later, the general had said something that stuck with Vex, maybe even more than he knew:

It's All
in the
Presentation

It's All in the Presentation

The next time your young child, grandchild or niece brings home a Rorschach painting from school, try an experiment. Instead of patting her on the head and saying, "Aren't you just the best little artist," try talking to your child about the specifics of the painting.

"Why did you use red here?" "What have you drawn here?" "What action is going on in this area?"

And then, when you praise the child and hang the painting on the refrigerator, use specifics, such as "I love how your flowers are turning toward the sun; that's very observant," or "You know, I don't know that I've ever seen scarier blue alien bugs." We guarantee that your little one will light up to such specific praise and remember it for a much longer time.

Author and scholar David Cherrington gives a fun demonstration of why such specificity is so important in his book *Rearing Responsible Children.*[16] Says Cherrington of a father he observed, "He expressed appreciation to each of his three children individually in the presence of his wife. The father's comment was a simple statement: 'I just want you to know how much I appreciate everything you do.' (The father supposed, like many managers, that any kind of positive praise would have a positive impact.)

"After he made the comment and left, his wife asked the child why the father had expressed appreciation. The ten-year-old replied, 'I guess he must be upset because I didn't get the dishes done like I was supposed to.' The thirteen-year-old replied, 'I don't know; I guess he was just feeling sentimental.' The fifteen-year-old said, 'Who knows what he meant. I don't think he understands what's going on around here.'"

In the work world, we've all known bosses who've fired out glibly, "Hey, buddy, you're doing a great job," or "I appreciate all you do," or "You sure look busy." Unfortunately, these hollow phrases often leave employees wondering, "Does this guy have any idea what I really do around here?"

And, yes, it is important to employees that we know what they are doing.

"Expressing appreciation in general, unspecified terms fails to communicate what the person did right and often appears insincere," says Cherrington. Instead, when giving praise, describe the great behavior, why it was helpful, and say thanks. It's that easy.

Mandy Assi, concierge manager at the Fairmont Royal York Hotel in Toronto, is a passionate practitioner of specific recognition. "Managers realize how hard it is to find good people, and that it's even more challenging to retain them—especially in [the hospitality] industry, where shift work can be difficult," she says.

"You need to be explicit. For example, I [recognize] you because I saw you checking in Mr. Smith. Mr. Smith was so upset, and you handled that with immense ease and calmed him down. Mr. Smith left with a big smile on his face. You also stayed late after your shift even though you were tired."

Does Assi's management style work? Just ask her eighteen employees. They nominated her for Royal York's Leader of the Quarter award, and even went to Assi's boss for his support in the nomination. "I have a lot of passion for my job, and to be recognized for something I love was amazing. I got a copy of all my team's [nominations], and knowing how much thought each person put into it means so much to me," Assi notes. She not only received the quarterly honor but was eventually honored as the hotel's Leader of the Year for 2000.

Managers like Assi know there are some simple keys for giving effective praise:

- Be timely.
- Be specific.
- Be sincere.
- Be prepared.

By taking a few minutes to prepare, and by using a few helpful techniques, your day-to-day recognition moments (and your formal recognition events) can do much more than simply thank employees for their contributions; they can enhance working relationships and increase feelings of loyalty and commitment.

Remember planting seeds in a paper cup during grade school? We learned early that plants require certain things, like sun, water and soil. Take away any of these factors and the plants don't do as well. In fact, they might not amount to anything at all. It's a good lesson for managers planting corporate carrots. Effective recognition involves certain key factors. Leave one out, and the experience just isn't as effective.

To ensure you've remembered everything, consider using the following mnemonic devices. The first is **CIA: the Company (and department), the Individual, the Award.** To recall this device, remember that a good presentation takes a little bit of investigative work.

Company: First, be prepared to talk about the company and team goals. You'll want to reiterate why this is a great place to work (your success, your history, exciting changes, superior quality, excellent customer service, or commitment to people, etc.). At FedEx, for example, managers use the recognition presentation as a time to talk about their values of people, service and profit. At KFC/Tricon, managers talk about their guiding operating principles of **C**leanliness, **H**ospitality, **A**ccuracy, **M**aintenance, **P**roduct, Quality and **S**peed (C.H.A.M.P.S.).

Individual: Next, relate specifically what the individual did to earn this award or recognition and how this achievement helps fulfill your team and company goals. To get the most impact, except with very shy recipients, you'll want to invite coworkers to talk about the person's qualities, creativity, dedication and/or specific work achievements.

At this point, you may want to consider another mnemonic device, **SAIL**, to tell a story. SAIL stands for: **Situation, Action, Impact** and **Link** to company values.

Remember the publisher commending his outstanding employee? The publisher told a wonderful story about Roger, using the following:

- Situation: (The problem or opportunity)
- Action: (What was done, in specific terms)
- Impact: (The result of the action)
- Link to Company Values: (How action contributed to company)

Award: Finally, you'll talk about what you are presenting to your employee—whether a formal award for service or performance or one of the informal ideas we talked about earlier (or hopefully one you thought up yourself). If a formal award, talk about the symbolism incorporated into the item (the gold company logo/emblem, the engraving, etc.).

And, of course, end with a sincere thank-you. With a little time, thought and effort—and maybe some help from these mnemonic devices—your carrot crop will never fail.

....

The great thing about carrots is that they're always in season. When times are good in your company, effective presentations will give you a chance to celebrate and reflect. Unlike monetary rewards that dry up when times are tight, carrots can be used during downturns to bring you closer together and give you hope that better times lie ahead. And by making the presentations public, you not only make the person being recognized feel appreciated, but also inspire those who are in attendance. In fact, a great presentation should get people asking themselves, "What memorable or noteworthy things have I done for the company?"

Here's an example of how it's done right. Grocery store chain Festival Foods in Onalaska, Wisconsin, invites customers and employees to "huddle up" for recognition moments.[17] Says president Dave Skogen, "While it's crucial to have the best quality products and the cleanest, most attractive facility, ultimately, it's employee attitude that brings customers back."

Twice a year, the company brings in all store directors for hands-on training and meetings called "Festival College." The company's training room has walls filled with quotes, including,

"People don't leave companies; they leave managers."

Recognition training became a course at the college, with face-to-face role-playing and instruction on points like:

- Know your people. "You have to do a little homework," says Skogen (yes, even the company president was trained). "You can't just walk out there and wing it."

- Ask others to say a few words about the employee's contributions. "Ask a coworker some questions," Skogen continues, "and even invite the coworker to say a few words. They'll know things about the associate that you don't. So the manager learns even more about the recipient."

- Let everyone who should attend know a few days in advance.

- Prepare, prepare, prepare. "Prepare, and spend some time on it, because it means more to the associate when you put more time into it than just a few minutes," notes customer service manager Heather Banaski.

- Make people accountable. Festival makes recognition huddle-ups a requirement for their managers—and although everyone says recognition is an event they look forward to, accountability ensures that an extra-busy manager doesn't ever let one of the company's most valuable human relations tools go unused.

After the training, leaders from the company offices go to

stores for regular presentations—not only to ensure recognition is being done right, but to get involved themselves and lead by example. Leaders attend—and participate in—every presentation they can when visiting stores.

Debbie Riggs of Tricon/KFC says their restaurants that do better at this type of public recognition also do markedly better in the financial side of their business. In fact, the connection between recognition and operational success is so important that recognition has become a key success criteria for supervisors and managers.

The recognition band, which celebrates employee achievements through peer recognition, has been a basic part of the company's recognition program for years. "I've seen people in tears when they get a visit from the recognition band. At the beginning, though, we had a senior executive who asked in a leadership meeting if 'we could do something about the band.' He felt it was noisy and distracting when he was on the phone. Our CEO stood up and said that the band was a reflection of our culture and it was here to stay."

Tricon/KFC leadership understands that it's okay to make a lot of noise about employee successes. Isn't it time you started walking to the beat of the recognition-band drummer?

What's the Frequency, Bugs?   How often do you give informal or formal recognition? Here are a few rules for a green thumb:

- **Verbal praise** or thanks should be given to every employee at least once a week. This does not always need to be in public, but it doesn't hurt if it's within earshot of other employees. Remember, thank them for specific actions that help achieve your department goals.

- **Informal rewards**—everything from handwritten cards to movie tickets, from spa trips to a free lunch—should typically be presented at least once a month to the people who create the most value and at least once a quarter to your core performers.

- **Formal rewards**—from company milestone awards to performance and service awards—should be presented at least annually to the majority of your team members. Most sophisticated companies we work with ensure that 40 percent of their workforce receives a formal award for outstanding performance at least once a year.

And these are just starting points. When it comes to corporate carrots, it's next to impossible to get too much of a good thing. Keep the rewards coming frequently, and you'll not only set a positive example for your employees but you'll also have help in recognizing. Employees who are recognized will begin to acknowledge each other and you.

CHALLENGE:

Come up with a fun tradition that you can start
for your employees. Some managers recognize
employee accomplishments with sets of walking teeth
(walking the talk), others with handwritten cards.
Whatever the tradition, keep it going and keep it fun.

SPACE *to* GROW

A FABLE · Part V

"Yes sir, planting those seeds was a good idea," Vex congratulated himself again as he slept in the bathtub late one morning a couple of weeks later. He glanced out the window at the sky. No clouds. It was going to be a scorcher. Wait, something was different. He could see out his windows. He sat up in the bathtub, and then walked outside for a closer look.

Sure enough, not only was the atmospheric dust missing from the vehicles, it also had been carefully wiped from all the office windows. He looked toward Lt. Tent's house. How long had this been going on? He wondered what else he had missed since he hadn't been out in his garden each morning. Suddenly, he felt a little out of touch. He walked out to his empty garden patch. From the hill, he noticed Lt. Atwork installing yet another measurement device. Was it his imagination, or did a few carrots put his people into overdrive?

CARROTS

He leaned back in his chair, grinning with pride, and then suddenly jerked forward. "Of course," he whispered, his eyes wide with surprise. It was frighteningly simple: Carrots were the key to success on Sub 3. They had the power to motivate people when everything else failed. He dug through the desk drawer and pulled out the second packet of carrot seeds. How many commanders before him had overlooked this small solution, leaving the colony in defeat?

With the seed packet still gripped tightly in his hand, Vex walked out and sat down, thunderstruck, on an empty garden row. His mind was racing as he set a goal for the improvements he wanted his staff to make. He needed to be more strategic with this second crop. Without taking time to change from his pajamas, he began planting the seeds. What a harvest this will be, he thought eagerly.

As he hastily tore open the packet, the front cover caught his eye. Under the picture of the faded orange carrot were some words. As he read them through the dirt and dust, they suddenly made perfect sense:

Keep Your Eye on the Harvest

Keep Your Eye on the Harvest

A Strategic Harvest

Of course, kindness is its own reward. But the best managers have discovered that if they direct their recognition toward certain goals, it makes employees more efficient and their work groups more productive.

Remember the story of Hansel and Gretel? They followed a trail of bread crumbs out of the woods and back to their home. Sometimes, with so much to do and so many competing programs and priorities, it's easy for even well-intentioned employees to get off track. By strategically leaving a trail of carrots, you can guide employees closer to the activities you value most.

The first step in this process is to set clear, specific goals in your team or department. And, as we all know, the most effective way to bring goals to your work team is to develop them by yourself and then communicate those values to your employees, right?

Of course not. That's a bit like a husband deciding to quit his job and open a fruit stand at the end of his driveway without consulting his wife or children. "Honey, I want us to be closer to nature and not so driven by material concerns," your spouse might say. "Well, that's fine," you might answer, "Bradley can do without braces. If he learns to cover his mouth when he speaks, no one will see the overbite. And Sarah doesn't need to go to college. I hear the mini mart is hiring."

Just like in families, very rarely will others buy into goals when they have not had a chance to contribute.

Now, there are many fine works on building a vision and mission for your company or team. We will not attempt to make this the definitive work on vision and values. But, briefly, here are a few simple tips for determining what is important to your team:

Know the macro. You must understand your company's overall corporate goals before you delve into the micro of your department or team goals. Get a copy of your company's credo and goals and start there. And when you are done with your team goals, go back to that document and make sure you are aligned.

Get your employees involved. By involving your employees in building the architecture of your team's future, you not only make them feel like valued owners, you gain the benefit of their knowledge. And they *will* have ideas you won't have, we guarantee. Of course, many of you are thinking, "If I involve my employees, I'll have to really live these values—every day." You are right. Too often, employees lose trust in a leader when they see a disconnect between what their manager says are her values and what she really does—her actions. She may claim to value "teamwork" but reward only her favorites for their individual performance. She may say she values "risk taking" but promotes only those people who don't make mistakes. But North America's most admired leaders live their values. And if you do, your employees will work harder for you and their trust level will skyrocket.

Figure out what you want to accomplish. Your vision should be an ideal image of the future. When you begin the goal-setting process, answer this simple question: "What do we want to accomplish?" Then consider these specifics:

- What do our clients value?
- What does the company value?
- What do our employees value?
- What is our basic purpose?
- What is our competitive situation?
- What will make us more productive, more valuable to our company, more efficient in the pursuit of our vision?

Keep it simple. Mission and vision statements focus you toward certain goals and away from others. Goals don't need to be complex. In fact, it's typically best to develop one simple, clear, driving vision, a handful of overall goals and then measurable, specific strategies for each goal. Strategies show us what we must do, in a specific time frame, to reach our goals. By way of example, a client service department may have an overall vision of "We provide the best customer service in our industry." A great over-

arching vision to steer toward, but pretty vague for most of our
employees. Thus, the team may create additional, more narrow
goals, including "Customers who call our service center will
receive satisfaction on the first call." That's getting better for the
front line. If they each pursue this goal, they won't let a customer
off the phone without finding them an answer. But effective strategies get even more specific. One strategy to help accomplish the
goal of "first-call satisfaction" might be "We answer all customer
calls within three rings." Another might be "A supervisor with full
decision-making power will be on the call floor at all times."

Post your values. Make sure your team's vision, goals and
strategies are posted in a conspicuous location. And make sure
every employee has a copy.

Hire people who embody your values. As you bring new
people into your team, make sure they can live your values and
goals. Make sure that as they are trained, they learn what is
important to your organization. If you're hiring for supervisory
or management positions, make sure they understand the value
of recognition—and know how to do it right.

Create victories along the way. Real change takes time. That's
why you must use carrots to recognize the right things in your
area, things that help move you toward your ultimate vision.
When individuals display heroics in living up to your strategies,

celebrate and provide a tangible award. Many companies we've worked with have developed "rite of passage" awards—like a wearable gold pin, a displayable certificate or a team jacket. You'll be amazed at the power these awards can have. You'll also be amazed at the power of presenting these awards in a formal setting. Especially when, in your celebration of the individual, you provide specific feedback that reinforces the right behaviors.

Many companies have also implemented team rewards when a group reaches a goal. This is a wonderful way to build morale.

As we said earlier, recognition of individuals should occur at least weekly. Team celebrations should occur at least every couple of months. Some people tell us, "It's okay, we have a great party at the end of the year. Our people love it." They may enjoy the free shrimp and beer—if they stick around long enough to attend. Chances are you're losing many of them during the year. Employees starved for recognition fall easy prey to competitors offering all-you-can-eat carrots.

CHALLENGE:

Sit down today and map out certain points throughout the coming year when your team may reach realistic group milestones. Then plan and budget for celebrations.

Carrots and credibility. Did you know that carrots can improve more than your eyesight? They can improve your credibility. That's important, because employee trust is nothing short of imperative if you want to get things done.

Carrots are hard evidence that your company vision and department goals are more than just a lot of talk. Carrots show that you believe the vision and goals can be attained, that you're not just giving them lip service. Carrots are proof that you are actively watching employee performance and there will be rewards for extra effort.

"More than anything, people want leaders who are credible," say leadership researchers Kouzes and Posner. "Credibility is the foundation of leadership. Period. Our findings are so consistent over such a long period of time that we've come to refer to this as the first law of leadership: if you don't believe the messenger, you won't believe the message."[18]

Which means you must not only develop values and goals, but you have to live them. You also must recognize those on your teams who embody those values. In short, you have to put your carrots where your mouth is. Stop talking about how important the values and goals are, and start recognizing progress towards them. The managers who do this find it an unparalleled source of competitive advantage. These managers also do not typically have to pay above-market rates for employees. Think about the best employers, companies that outperform their peers—companies like Southwest Airlines, FedEx, Tricon, Johnson & Johnson. They make employees feel good about their accomplishments. They build the self-esteem of their people. They show their people that they matter.

That kind of environment is possible in your team. Even without a powerhouse CEO or wonderful overall corporate culture, you can create the type of work group where people are committed and loyal. It begins with a guiding vision, achievable goals and specific strategies that have buy-in from employees.

It begins with a 24-carrot manager.

Labor Pains   If you manage a unionized workforce, you know that carrots can carry a degree of risk. We know from firsthand experience that managers may start using rewards in unionized settings—getting employees to go beyond regular job requirements—only to hear from unhappy union leadership.

While research strongly supports the notion that reward programs in unionized environments have a positive impact on productivity, Nancy Mills, executive director of the AFL-CIO Working for America Institute, says, "If an incentive program is just making workers work faster and the only ones that can do it are a small percentage, then there is a problem."[19]

Indeed, favoritism is frowned upon in most labor settings. Says Mills, "Incentives that recognize only a few individuals are problematic ... and fail to acknowledge the contributions of a wider group."

Here are a few guidelines for improving the manager-union employee relationship and delivering recognition to unionized teams:

Communicate early. Discuss with your team what rewards you plan to offer and how this is an addition to, not an infringement of, their compensation package. Let your employees air their views before you hand out the first carrot. If the recognition is going to be formal—as in a safety award, performance award, service award, etc.—begin negotiations early with your union representatives so rewards can be handed out in a fair and equitable manner.

sidelight continued ☛

Give employees a voice. Let employee teams have a role in choosing reward recipients. Once a week or once a month, gather a small group together to identify those worthy of rewards.

Reward groups of employees. Instead of rewarding just the best individual, and instead of trying to reward your entire workforce, provide an appropriate reward to a three- or four-person team that completes a special project, achieves an accident-free record, develops a new process or in some other way advances the organization's goals.

Don't forget the free stuff. To get the most from your people and to honor their contributions, don't ignore the simple things you can do every day. Recognize your employees with your words, i.e., "Libby, thank you for taking care of that patient's billing problem so efficiently," or "Mike, great job in helping your new teammate learn his role." Or give a handwritten note of appreciation or a card of thanks. Research shows that committed employees receive praise and recognition from their immediate supervisor at least once every seven days.

No matter where they're planted, carrots are jam-packed with everything you need to build a happy, productive workforce—and a successful, effective manager. A little planning and forethought will ensure that they flourish in your corporate culture.

SPACE *to* GROW

A FABLE · Part VI

It seemed to take an eternity for the second crop of carrots to mature. As he cultivated his carrot crop, Vex watched for specific behaviors in his staff—behaviors that moved people closer to his overall goals. Then he rewarded those behaviors. And sure enough, his people focused on the rewarded behaviors.

He even began to use what he'd learned with carrots to improve the base's formal recognition ceremonies for years of service and special performance, when awards were provided by the home base. On many planets, these ceremonies had become tired and rather dull. Some planets had stopped holding the ceremonies altogether and just stuck the formal award in the person's mail slot.

CARROTS

But Vex decided to spice up the formal recognition a little. When a service anniversary or promotion occurred, he called a group meeting. He asked other base members to comment on the performance of the individual being honored, and Vex even prepared a few remarks in advance. He made the events celebrations, and now his people actually looked forward to their service anniversaries and other formal recognition events. As one lieutenant asked, "Who wouldn't like a day when the entire team gathers and shares their favorite work memories of you?"

As Vex noted in his personal log:

Make Formal Milestones Moments Worth Remembering

Make Formal Milestones Moments Worth Remembering

Picture Olympic champion Bonnie Blair standing on the medal podium. Or Roberto Benigni bounding to the podium to receive his Oscar. These are examples of formal recognition at its best.

We've seen this type of emotion and impact in corporate settings.

Says one friend of ours, "When I received my ten-year service award, I was asked, 'Can you go to the loading dock to pick it up?' When I received my fifteen-year award, I was working for someone else. They invited my husband in; coworkers gathered. It was a meaningful recognition event with a wonderful award. My boss cooked me breakfast and they all talked about projects we had worked on together."

Think employees don't remember the times they were—or, worse, were not—recognized by their bosses? Think again. Employees may crave carrots, but they have the memories of elephants. And an elephant never forgets.

When we were presenting to a group of managers in Philadelphia recently, a man approached us after the talk. He said, "My grandfather often talked about an award he received for his thirty-year service anniversary. You know what happened?"

We shook our heads.

"The CEO got his name wrong. Can you believe that? It affected him for years afterward."

Think about this: The story was being told to us by the man's grandson. The tale of misery had already been passed down two generations.

Does a formal recognition moment make a significant impact? You'd better believe it.

But presenting a formal award like a service, performance, sales or safety award doesn't have to be a burden; it can be an opportunity—to bond an employee to you and your team and to reinforce your goals and vision. All it takes is a little preparation, sincerity and specificity (remember the tips we gave you on good presentations on page 72).

But, of course, formal recognition can't stand alone.

Let us repeat that.

Formal awards must be supported by day-to-day recognition. After all, if you've fed your employees a steady diet of prunes all year, will they react well to suddenly receiving a formal carrot? As one employee once told us, "It's hard to celebrate if you've been beaten up on the way to the party."

CHALLENGE:

Check with your HR department to find out
when your next employee will receive his or her
service award. About a week before,
spend a few minutes preparing remarks
and asking coworkers to speak.
Make this employee's day special,
and your investment in time and energy
will come back to you tenfold.

SPACE *to* GROW

A FABLE · Part VII

With the formal and day-to-day carrot presentations, before his eyes Vex's team was moving closer and closer to his goal, his harvest.

Then a strange thing happened: as his garden grew, so did requests from people to join the settlement on Sub 3. They came from friends of his workers. Apparently, his people had expressed how committed they were to their current assignment, how they felt appreciated and part of the team. The new arrivals brought needed skills and abilities to Sub 3, and the environment began to change for the better.

"Thanks to the efforts and innovation of our environmental team, I am proud to report the total eradication of large, disgusting roaches on Colony Sub 3," Vex wrote in a transmission on the anniversary of his arrival. "And environmental dust has been decreased by 84 percent."

Soon, Vex and Sub 3 began to attract some of the best and brightest of all the cadets. And it wasn't long until his success came to the attention of his superiors. After a close inspection, the generals still could not understand what he was doing differently. Even his people couldn't put their fingers on the difference.

But Vex could. He put a small note on his desk, next to his letters of commendation and promotions. It said:

Keep
On
Growing

SPACE *to* GROW

A FABLE · Part VIII · The End

Captain Vex determined never to be without a carrot crop again.

CHALLENGE:

Close the book—and call in your first employee!

SEVEN SHORT WAYS TO BUILD COMMITMENT CHECKLIST

Creating a fairy-tale work environment begins with recognition. Your employees need it more than they need money, perks, or titles.

To recap, here are seven short things we've learned about recognition. Remember these, and your employees may just start whistling while they work:

☐ 1. NO PAIN, NO GAIN.

The CEO, the big corporate culture, or financial rewards will not make your division or team successful. It may be difficult at first, but it really is up to you. The good news: Recognition is one thing that's completely in your control.

☐ 2. Carrots improve your eyesight.

Noticing and recognizing the right behaviors is the key to strengthening employee relationships in any economy. As your workforce shrinks and you need to do more with less, keeping quality employees becomes even more critical. As a manager, it's your job to recognize and bond your most valued people to your company. And you must also help direct and motivate your core performers.

☐ 3. Pick your carrots wisely.

Remember the saying "Money can't buy everything"? Well, it's true. Don't wait until you can offer an employee a raise or promotion. Real thanks is its own reward. In numerous surveys of work satisfaction, top on employee lists is "feeling appreciated." In fact, when employees feel recognized and involved, they are much less likely to keep asking about money. There are some relatively simple things you can do that will earn big returns. For example, remember your employees' birthdays and work anniversaries; find out what inexpensive rewards they value (for example, tickets to a ball game or a few hours off to spend with their kids). Walk around your department every day, talk to your people (gulp!) and thank them—sincerely and often.

☐ 4. IT'S ALL IN THE PRESENTATION.

Praise and recognition must be specific to have an impact.
General praise like "You do great work" can actually have
the opposite effect, leaving your employees wondering,
"Does he have any idea what I really do around here?"
In private and public recognition moments, specific praise
links individual accomplishments to company goals. For
example, "Cheryl, I noticed the way you handled that customer complaint. Great work. As you know, we value quick
resolutions of problems as one of our core strategies."

☐ 5. MAKE FORMAL MILESTONES WORTH REMEMBERING.

Make the most of your company's formal corporate
awards—service, safety and others—with a powerful group
presentation. Presenting a formal award doesn't have to be
a burden, it can be an opportunity to bond an employee
to you and your team and to reinforce your goals and
vision. All it takes is a little preparation, sincerity and
specificity.

☐ 6. KEEP YOUR EYE ON THE HARVEST.

Focus recognition on the kinds of behaviors that make your team and company better. When you are strategic, your employees will understand that recognition is not a popularity contest but an important tool to move people toward specific goals, make employees more efficient and make work groups more productive.

☐ 7. KEEP ON GROWING.

Recognition means most to an employee when it's sincere and spontaneous. Some form of recognition should occur at least every seven days. So if you wait until a year-end party or an annual review, you are waiting much too long to recognize and are probably losing people along the way.

Neglect can be a poisoned apple. Recognition is the elixir that will spark better attitudes and performance. Says Jeffrey Pfeffer, a professor of organizational behavior at Stanford University, "The [financial] returns from managing people in ways that build high commitment . . . are typically on the order of 30 to 50 percent."[20]

So take a hard look in the mirror and ask yourself how you can recognize the fairest of them all. Learn to recognize your employees for their efforts, thank them often, and reward their achievements. You can awaken them from their anger and apathy and they will fall in love with their jobs again.

And chances are, you'll work together happily ever after.

ENDNOTES:

1. "High Turnover," *Human Resource Executive*, September 2000.

2. "How Happy Are Your Employees?" *The Kiplinger Letter*, 7 September 2001.

3. See Daniel Horne, "Retain Employees During the Boom," *Potentials*, January 2001.

4. "More Employers Emphasizing Non-Monetary Rewards to Attract and Retain Talent," Watson Wyatt News & Issues release, quoting survey of 410 employers in the fifth annual Watson Wyatt Strategic Rewards® survey, 18 December 2000.

5. See L. Belkin, "Life's Work," *New York Times*, 31 January 2001.

6. See Jack Welch, Letter to Shareholders, 26 February 2001.

7. The Conference Board, *HR Executive Review*: Employee Recognition Programs, 1999.

8. See J. M. Kouzes and B. Z. Posner, *Encouraging the Heart*. San Francisco: Jossey-Bass, 1999.

9. See M. Buckingham and C. Coffman, *First, Break All the Rules*. New York: Simon & Schuster, 1999.

10. See R. K. Miller, "The Right Package," *Human Resource Executive*, December 2000.

11. See *Potentials*, December 2000, quoting American Express Incentive Services "Achieve More" Survey.

12. "Perk of the Month," *Human Resource Executive*, July 2001.

13. See "Recognition, First Strategy at Every Last Resort," *Kudos* 5, no. 3.

14. "Perk of the Month," *Human Resource Executive*, January 2001.

15. See D. Fonville, "Hungry for Productivity?" *Richmond Times-Dispatch*, 1 April 2000.

16. See David Cherrington, *Rearing Responsible Children*. Salt Lake City: Deseret Book, 1993.

17. See "Recognition, That's on Aisle 4," *Kudos* 5, no. 4.

18. See J. M. Kouzes and B. Z. Posner, *Encouraging the Heart*. San Francisco: Jossey-Bass, 1999.

19. See J. Casison and T. Benitez, "Division of Labor," *Incentive*, September 2000.

20. See Jeffrey Pfeffer, *The Human Equation*, Harvard Business School Press, Boston, 1998.

ABOUT THE AUTHORS

Adrian Gostick and **Chester Elton** are the authors of the successful *Managing with Carrots: Using Recognition to Attract and Retain the Best People*, published in 2001 by Gibbs Smith, Publisher, and nominated as the Society for Human Resource Management Book of the Year. As motivation experts, the authors have been guests on CNN Television, Bloomberg Television and National Public Radio.

Adrian lives with his wife, Jennifer, and son, Tony, in Oakley, Utah.

Chester lives with his wife, Heidi, and their four children in Summit, New Jersey.

REVIEWS OF *MANAGING WITH CARROTS*

"*Managing with Carrots* is the rarest of books: a lively, enjoyable read that dispenses practical, valuable business advice. For organizations facing the critical challenge of finding and retaining the best employees—and who isn't?—this book provides a step-by-step approach to achieving enhanced loyalty and commitment through strategic, integrated employee recognition. It's a must read for anyone in leadership."

Donna Oldenburg, Publisher, *Incentive* magazine

"This fine book is filled with extremely useful information: case studies, statistics, survey results and excellent advice to leaders. I would recommend it to anyone who is in a leadership role and to all recognition professionals. The authors have taken reams of data and reduced it to an elegantly simple guidebook for anyone who cares about attracting and retaining top talent. Bravo!"

**Dee Hansford, President, *Dee Hansford Consulting*
Former Manager of Cast Recognition,
Walt Disney World Resort**

"*Managing with Carrots* is an excellent work that deserves serious attention from business leaders seeking to enhance employee retention and productivity. The authors effectively draw on relevant data and proven principles of effective management, while delivering a very readable and practical guide to creating and pursuing an effective employee recognition strategy."

Steven C. Wheelwright, *Edsel Bryant Ford Professor Emeritus*, Former Senior Associate Dean, Harvard Business School

"The authors' knowledge combined with very up-to-date research gives this book strong credibility. The most valuable elements of this book are the charts, statistics, brief corporate examples and lists of ideas on how to grow a carrots crop in your organization. These bits of information would be excellent fodder for a presentation on recognition in your own company."

Gina Matesic, Book Review Editor, *HRProfessional* magazine

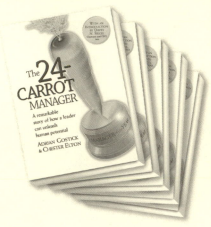

NOTES

NOTES

NOTES

NOTES

NOTES

NOTES